The Birds We Live With

The Birds We Live With

Catherine E. Clark

Lower Valley Road Atglen, Pennsylvania 19310

Designed by John P. Cheek
Cover design by Bruce Waters
Type set in Bradley Hand ITC/Zurich BT
ISBN: 978-0-7643-3260-9
Printed in China

Schiffer Books are available at special discounts for bulk purchases for sales promotions or premiums. Special editions, including personalized covers, corporate imprints, and excerpts can be created in large quantities for special needs. For more information contact the publisher:

Published by Schiffer Publishing Ltd.
4880 Lower Valley Road
Atglen, PA 19310
Phone: (610) 593-1777; Fax: (610) 593-2002
E-mail: Info@schifferbooks.com

For the largest selection of fine reference books on this and related subjects, please visit our web site at www.schifferbooks.com
We are always looking for people to write books on new and related subjects. If you have an idea for a book please contact us at the above address.

This book may be purchased from the publisher.
Include $5.00 for shipping.
Please try your bookstore first.
You may write for a free catalog.

In Europe, Schiffer books are distributed by
Bushwood Books
6 Marksbury Ave.
Kew Gardens
Surrey TW9 4JF England
Phone: 44 (0) 20 8392 8585; Fax: 44 (0) 20 8392 9876
E-mail: info@bushwoodbooks.co.uk
Website: www.bushwoodbooks.co.uk

CONTENTS

INTRODUCTION

I've been illustrating a weekly newspaper column about birds for about seven years now. I have two notebooks full of drawings, adding up to a whopping ten inches thick. Going through and trying to pick out my favorites was tough. Turns out almost all of them are my favorites.

Birds have always been favorite subjects for my paintings. Looking back to early photos of my art shows in Binghamton, New York, back in the (hmmm, I'm not sure I actually want to admit this) 70s, I see lots of bird paintings in my line up.

The column I've been illustrating is "Ask the Bird Folks," written by Mike O'Connor for the *Cape Codder* newspaper. Mike owns a birding shop on Cape Cod in Massachusetts. He answers all kinds of questions about birds, bird watching, bird feeding, bird seed, bird migration, bird droppings ... well, you get it. Questions come from all across the country and even other parts of the world.

One day Peter Schiffer of Schiffer Books approached me and said, "We think your drawings are endearing and should be in a book. What do you think?" After they came in with the Jaws of Life to lift my jaw off the floor, I replied, "Okay, sure."

I get to pick a mix of my black and white illustrations and my color paintings. I hope people will want to take a look. But my bigger hope is to inspire folks to take a look out their window, maybe take a stroll and actually see what is around, and maybe, just maybe, take some small action to save what they see.

BIRDS OF THE BACK YARD

Books like to have titles and categories. This is tough when it comes to birds. There is a lot of overlapping. Feeder birds, birds that will come to a bird feeder, can be backyard birds. But not all backyard birds are feeder birds. Woodland birds can also be backyard birds. See what I mean?

The point is that birds are everywhere for us to enjoy. How far you take it is up to you.

A couple years ago an article appeared in *U.S. News and World Report*, entitled "50 Ways to Improve Your Life." Bird watching was number #46 on the list after things like "clean your closet," "quit your job," and "grow a plant." Most of those sound a bit too risky to me, especially growing a plant...that means you have to remember to water it.

Birding (the cool, hip way to refer to bird watching) has become a $10 billion a year industry. The great thing about birding is that you don't have to spend a dime or the sky's the limit. You can go crazy with the latest optics, the latest squirrel-proof feeders, the latest look in Gortex, or not.

Feeder Birds

The best way to see birds up close is to put out a feeder. At the left are a few birds that will come to a feeder. From the top down are the Black-capped Chickadee, Tufted Titmouse, Ruby-Throated Hummingbird, a Downy Woodpecker, and a Northern Cardinal.

These illustrations were all done in watercolor for a series of my own prints and note cards.

The Ruby-Throated Hummingbird requires a special nectar feeder which I will talk about later.

BLACK-CAPPED CHICKADEE

For fun in the backyard, nothing beats the Black-capped Chickadee. Put a feeder out with some sunflower, the chickadee will be the first to check it out. Put up a birdhouse, a chickadee will probably be the first to move in. For its size, the Black-capped Chickadee has a lot of personality. With a bit of patience, chickadees will come to your hand to nab a sunflower seed. The drawing below was for an article about this.

On Cape Cod, where I live, there is a park where you can go to with some sunflower seed. Just hold it out and a chickadee will be there within minutes. Less than a minute.

The painting, right, was done with acrylic paint on canvas paper. I like experimenting with different textured surfaces. Canvas paper still gives a look of canvas but allows the paint to go on more smoothly. I then scanned the painting into the computer to make my own prints and note cards. Equipment is so good now and so affordable, that everyone can have fun with this. You can actually see the canvas texture of the original painting.

The bottom right chickadee started as a black & white illustration which I then colorized on the computer using a drawing tablet. Just something I was having fun with.

9

Birds show up at feeders during nesting season when they gather worms and bugs to feed their young, as the chickadee is demonstrating.

It is not often that I get to portray a bird in a "cartoony" way for "Ask the Bird Folks," but when I do, I often choose the chickadee.

Sometimes I keep the bird real for a cartoon. This drawing was for a question about catching bird flu from feeder birds (you won't!)

The painting, right, was done with acrylic on a piece of roofing slate, my preferred surface. My favorite step is the background. I slop on a bunch of different colors, wait until just the right time between the paint being wet and dry, and then brush in a criss-cross technique.

The background color was achieved with Mars Black, Pthalo Blue, Raw Umber, Alizarin Crimson, and Titanium White. These are also pretty much the colors I have slopped on every article of clothing I own.

The drawing, left, was done to go with an article about birds' bathroom habits. Yes, it's hard to believe, but someone actually did have a question about bird pee.

BLUE JAY

Nothing beats having these guys in your backyard. They're colorful, raucous, and "in your face." The Northern Cardinal often gets the nod as the most colorful bird, but take a close look at the beautiful blue hues of a Blue Jay and you'll think twice.

Blue Jays often get a bad rap as being bullies of the backyard feeder. Folks often ask how to keep them off. Hard to believe. They do have this interesting behavior of filling their cheeks with seed, similar to a chipmunk. Bird shops selling seed don't mind that.

Like many birds, animals, and humans, they do steal and consume the occasional egg from another bird's nest.

This illustration was done in my usual method of combining pen and ink with pencil work.

The Top left was a very early drawing, done in straight pen and ink, to which I later added some pencil work.

AMERICAN GOLDFINCH

Goldfinches add a dash of bright color to the backyard bird feeder. They come to feeders year round, but in the winter they turn a dull, olive green.

The best way to attract these guys is by putting out a thistle feeder. It has small holes so that the seed, which is actually Nyger seed, doesn't just fall out.

The painting, right, is another one done on a piece of roofing slate. I was trying to stay a bit more loose and less detailed. It was more practice than anything, but it's turned out to be a popular print for me.

The drawing, far left, is an early illustration for "Ask the Bird Folks," done in straight forward pen and ink, which is the way the newspaper required it back then. The one on the right has been colorized on the computer.

WHITE-BREASTED NUTHATCH

The nuthatch will come to a feeder, but just take a look around. Chances are that you'll see one headed down a tree trunk like a little wind-up toy, looking for bugs under the bark. Its unmistakable "aank aank" call sounds like it's always annoyed at something.

The watercolor, left, started out as practice. I'm afraid of watercolor. I love it, but I don't quite know what to do with it. This little practice painting turned out pretty well.

The nuthatch, right, was done with acrylic on canvas paper.

TUFTED TITMOUSE

The Tufted Titmouse ranks up close to the Black-capped Chickadee for cuteness and personality. They will readily come to a feeder of sunflower and, with a little patience, will also come to your hand.

This was done with that scary watercolor medium. I think I'm getting the hang of it.

Clark

EASTERN BLUEBIRD

The bluebird is the most sought-after bird to attract to the backyard. It used to be that the right habitat and a big open space with a birdhouse were the only ways to bring them near. And thanks to people doing just that, the Eastern Bluebird has made a huge comeback.

Other than putting out a source of water, there was not much you could do. They ate berries and insects. But that was then.

An extraordinary change has occurred; the Eastern Bluebird has become a feeder bird. It's almost like evolution happening right before our very eyes.

Bluebirds now readily come to feeders containing sunflower hearts and suet. You can even offer them mealworms which are available live or roasted. The live mealworms require a feeder with an edge so the worms don't crawl out. Specially designed feeders are now made just for bluebirds, requiring them to go inside, to keep other birds from getting the food first.

There are more bluebirds here on Cape Cod in the winter than in the summer. They winter here in flocks. It is not uncommon to look out and see a bunch on your feeder or birdbath.

If the bluebirds in these two drawings look like the ones to the left, you are right. Thanks to the world of digital wizardry I can use a bird I like in more than one drawing. Sometimes the time constraints of meeting a newpaper deadline require a shortcut.

In the early days of doing these drawings I would turn to good old "White-Out" to make a correction. And it was pretty common that what my boss had in mind did not match what I drew. The computer has saved my hair from getting any grayer than it is. Just in the nick of time.

A bluebird box requires a hole with a diameter of 1-1/2 inches. This one is shown with a metal "toothbender." It protects the hole from being chewed or pecked larger by another critter.

All birdhouses should be able to be opened for cleaning. This should be done after each nesting cycle, or at least in the spring prior to use.

NORTHERN CARDINAL

The Northern Cardinal is the supreme bird of all the birds people want to attract to their yards.

It is pretty easy. Sunflower seed is their favorite, but they also seem to love safflower seed. I've been helping people attract birds to their yards for quite some time; twenty years to be exact. It's frustrating to hear people say, "My dad gets out the BB gun when he sees a squirrel at the feeder." My goal has always been to get folks to appreciate and enjoy all the wildlife they attract.

The easiest way to discourage squirrels at a feeder is to offer safflower seed. The birds, especially cardinals, seem to love it. But squirrels don't like it at all, and grackles, another bird people don't want around for whatever reason, don't either.

At the same time every year the calls start coming in about a strange bird people start seeing in their yards. "I looked out my window and something that looked like a small vulture was on my feeder."

Birds molt every year. They hunker down and lie low during this time until it's over. They look very strange during this transition, especially the Northern Cardinal. With its bald, black head, it does, indeed, look like a tiny vulture.

One thing to keep in mind is that cardinals like to feed from a tray, a feeder with any kind of edge, or the ground. They do not usually come to the perch of a tube feeder.

This painting was originally of the cardinal, only, on slate. The chickadees are actually just one chickadee from another painting. The Downy Woodpecker is from a painting on canvas. Each painting was scanned separately into my computer.

I played around with the arrangement on the computer until I came up with a pleasing scene. Pretty neat and fun.

I use a Wacom tablet when working with images. I switch between Adobe Photoshop and Corel Photopaint.

19

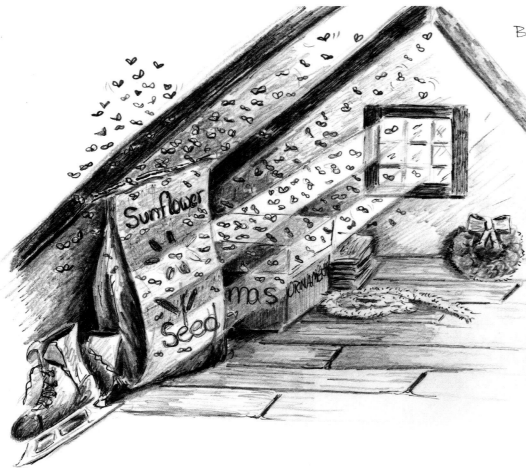

BIRD SEED & BIRD FEEDING ETIQUETTE

You know that not-quite-empty carton of milk, with an expiration date that expired three months ago, sitting in the back of your refrigerator? Go ahead, take a drink. No? Hmmm. But we think birds will want to eat that seed we got on sale and stocked up on last spring. And it's now the middle of winter!

Bird seed should not be stored for more than two months, and not even that long if it has been really hot. It should definitely not be kept in your house. If you do, you'll be chasing meal moths around for the rest of your life… or until you move. Moth eggs and larva are in all seed and, if kept long enough, they will hatch. It's no different than if you leave a box of oatmeal sitting around long enough. There really is no reason to get more bird seed than you'll use up within a couple of weeks to a month. Keep it stored in a cool, dry location. A metal trash can works well and will keep out little critters like mice and chipmunks.

Wash your feeders! Take them apart and soak them in a little dish soap. Add a bit of bleach if they're really icky and moldy. RINSE WELL. Let them dry thoroughly.

Tip:

When you go on vacation, bring your feeders inside. Otherwise, a bird will waste energy trying to get one seed and may even get stuck! The birds won't hate you and will come back when you put your feeder out again.

A good feeder has a plastic baffle insert to keep seed from going all the way to the bottom where birds can't get at it and the seed will just rot.

Don't be lazy! Don't put new seed on top of old! Put the old seed in a can, put in the new seed, and rotate the old seed to the top (remember that milk?). Otherwise your feeder will end up with a bottom full of cement or some weird science experiment.

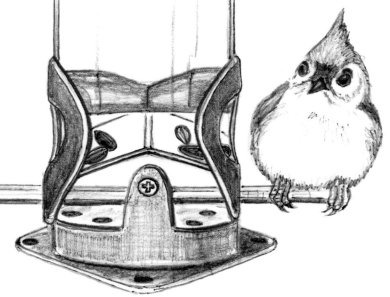

Keeping a fresh source of water will attract even more birds to your yard. Clean your bath thoroughly with a little dishsoap, a good brush and a hose. If the bath becomes discolored over time, don't worry about it. It won't hurt the birds.

There are products on the market to add to birdbath water to keep the bath clean. Folks ask all the time about the safety of these products. We tell them to read the label. It clearly states not safe for human consumption. If it's not safe for a big human being, how can it be safe for a tiny chickadee?

Get yourself a good brush, keep the water fresh, and don't worry about any discoloration of your birdbath. The birds won't judge you and they'll appreciate not drinking a bunch of chemicals.

An open source of fresh water can be hard to find for birds in the dead of winter. Robins especially love a birdbath in the winter. It's not uncommon to look out the window and see a flock of them on the bath.

Add a heater to your bath in the winter and the birds will love it. And no, it will not electrocute them or burn them.

22

This drawing was done for an article about throwing rice at weddings. The idea that birds will eat the rice and blow up into blimps is a myth. However, the new, trendy tradition does seem to be to throw bird seed. And what new bride wouldn't love having a chickadee trying to grab a sunflower seed stuck in her hair?

The question was about putting out stale, white bread for birds. Not the best choice for long-term nutrition, for birds or humans, but won't hurt them.

This drawing was for an article about birds eating berries. This is an example of my vision not matching my boss's. It got the ax.

RUBY-THROATED HUMMINGBIRD

The Ruby-throated Hummingbird is the smallest hummingbird in North America and the only hummingbird east of the Mississippi.

The male is easily identified by the colorful red throat patch.

The hummingbird is also a backyard feeder bird. However, it is not attracted to bird seed. It is attracted to a sugar-water solution which requires a special feeder specifically designed for hummingbirds.

This drawing was to emphasize how small a hummingbird's nest is by comparing it to a quarter.

24

Now for the bad news. You know that fancy, round glass humming-bird feeder your Aunt Edna bought you for Christmas? It's going to leak. There's some law of physics going on here that can't be explained and can't be solved. Fancy round feeders with the long tube sticking out the bottom leak. Period. So put Aunt Edna's feeder away and save it in case she comes visiting in the summer.

Flat hummingbird feeders, like the one left, usually come completely apart, making them easy to clean. This is important because the feeder needs to be cleaned every three to four days. Glass tube type feeders, like on the previous page, are good too, but you may need a feeder brush to really get it clean.

Usually a hummingbird feeder will have enough red on it to attract the birds. Adding food coloring is old school. It is now thought that adding food coloring is not healthy for the birds.

You can spend a bunch of money on a tiny box of powder to dissolve into water or make your own. It's really complicated, though. Dissolve one part sugar, into four parts water. Even I can do it. Use table sugar only. And never use honey.

The hummer, left, is my favorite. It seemed that the feeder needed to be dripping on something and I added this ornery little hummer as an afterthought.

25

Bees are attracted to hummingbird feeders too. There is not much you can do about it. You can bring the feeder in until they go away or you can put up a second feeder to try and please everybody.

I did not intend to give bees a bad rap by making them look so big and scary in this drawing. They're just trying to earn a living too. However, I couldn't resist giving it the look of an old sci-fi horror film.

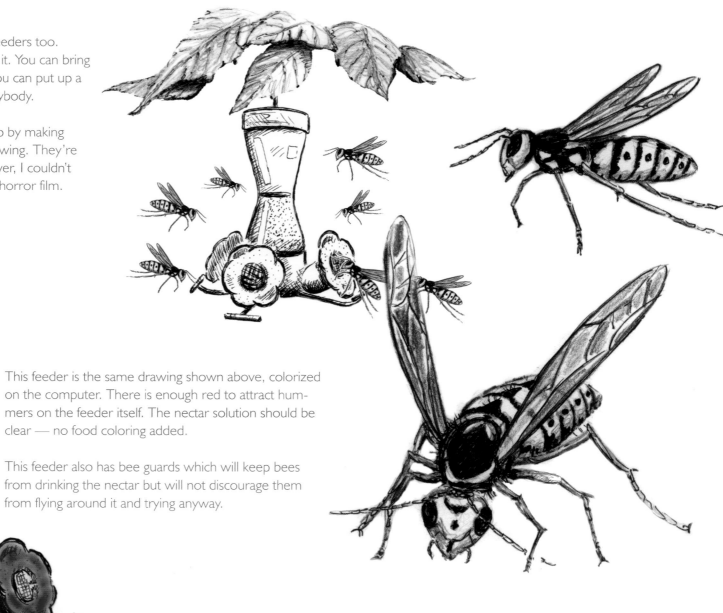

This feeder is the same drawing shown above, colorized on the computer. There is enough red to attract hummers on the feeder itself. The nectar solution should be clear — no food coloring added.

This feeder also has bee guards which will keep bees from drinking the nectar but will not discourage them from flying around it and trying anyway.

Tiny hummingbirds migrate all the way down to Central America. Someone heard a myth that hummingbirds will sometimes hitch a ride on the backs of migrating geese and wondered if there was any truth to it. The answer is no.

A few more hummer tidbits:

• It would take five hummingbirds to equal the weight of one chickadee.

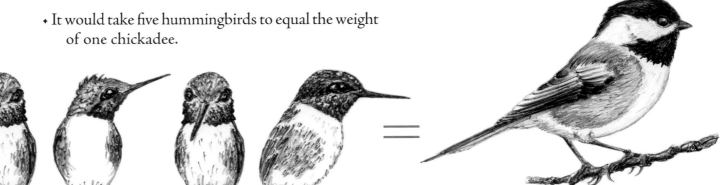

• Hummers also feed on small insects, including spiders.

• Hummers have very long tongues to reach down tubular flowers to reach nectar.

• Hummers are the only birds that can hover and fly backwards.

• Hummers can flap their wings approximately 75 times per second.

• Hummers are fiesty and will fight with bumblebees over a flower.

• The Sphinx Moth is commonly mistaken for a hummingbird.

NORTHERN ORIOLE

Northern Orioles can also be attracted to a backyard by putting out a nectar feeder. A feeder for them, however, must have perches.

Cutting an orange in half will also bring them in. The orange half can be skewered to a special holder or just stuck on a nail in a tree.

Orioles create elaborate, hanging nests. They will be happy to help themselves to short pieces of yarn or string put out in a suet holder or along a fence rail.

Woodpeckers

Woodpeckers are the natural landscapers of our backyards. Unlike the deafening, annoying mechanical sounds of weed wackers, lawn mowers, and now the dreaded leaf blowers (grab a rake and get some exercise for crying out loud), the thrumming sound of a woodpecker on a nearby tree is comforting and soothing.

Although woodpeckers will excavate a nesting site in live trees, many prefer dead trees, dead branches, and rotten stumps. After a woodpecker is done with his nest, something else will often move in. Unless a dead tree or branch threatens to harm you or your house, consider leaving it. It will be well used by grateful inhabitants.

DOWNY WOODPECKER

The Downy Woodpecker is the woodpecker most commonly seen in our backyards. It is the smallest woodpecker in the United States and Canada. It can be seen spiraling up a tree or around a branch. The male has a red patch on the back of the head. It will come to suet and peanuts.

HAIRY WOODPECKER

The Hairy Woodpecker looks very much like a large Downy. The beak is quite a bit longer on a Hairy and its outer white tail feathers have no markings, while the Downy's tail feathers have a series of black markings. The Hairy favors forests and woods and will come to suet and peanuts.

The Hairy Woodpecker (bottom) is larger than the Downy Woodpecker (top), with a much longer beak.

29

"Why is a woodpecker pecking my house?" This is a question we hear a lot, especially in the spring.

Sometimes the woodpecker simply wants to announce its territory or attract a mate by making a lot of noise and will peck at a metal chimney guard or flashing. This usually does not cause damage, it is using your house like a giant bulletin board.

On the other hand, it is thought that woodpeckers can actually hear insects under bark or under your shingles or in rotten wood and trim. If this is the case, they may attempt to locate a tasty snack by drilling a few holes. Or the woodpecker may just be looking for a new home (all the more reason to let that dead tree remain on your property).

If I want to add a touch of color, I'll often do it on the computer using a graphics tablet. I'll also sometimes use the same bird for more than one article, using the computer to add it to a new background. The Downy above and left is the same drawing.

Other Backyard Woodpeckers

There is no better group than woodpeckers to hone your observation skills. Whether you're an artist, a birder, or just want to know these fabulous creatures better, creating quick sketches of these guys will help to develop your eye for detail.

Instead of immediately going for the field guide when you see a bird you don't recognize, jot down in a notebook what you see.

Is the beak long or short? Is there color on the bird; if so, where? Are the tail feathers all the same color or are the outer tail feathers different? Is the chest a solid color, stripes, or spots?

Start with the some basic oval shapes for the body and head and go from there. Just go with simple lines and stay loose. It doesn't need to be perfect. Make it a habit to note the date, time, maybe the weather, and what the bird was doing. In time, you'll have a neat nature diary that will be fun to look through as you get better. And you will get better.

Yellow-bellied
Sapsucker

Red-headed
Woodpecker

Northern Flickers are often seen
on the ground hunting ants.

31

IVORY-BILLED WOODPECKER

The chronology of the demise of the Ivory-Billed Woodpecker and reports of its possible rediscovery would make for a riveting "CSI" episode.

The best place to read about this bird's history and an up-to-date account of searches and reported sightings is on the internet at http://Wikipedia.org. If you don't own a computer, get one. If you don't know how to access information on the internet, ask your kid.

The Ivory-Billled Woodpecker was, or maybe is, the largest woodpecker in the United States. Here's the best part—due to logging of its habitat and hunting by collectors it was considered extinct in the 1800s. When a pair was sighted in Florida in 1920, they were shot for specimens! Of course.

An expedition led by the Cornell Lab of Ornithology to the Big Woods in Arkansas in 2004 and 2005 led to the newsworthy report that an Ivory-Billed had been sighted. Another team went in during 2006. Even though none of the evidence can be confirmed and the debate continues, hope also remains. Enough so that Cornell and The Nature Conservancy bought up huge tracts of land to add to the Big Woods habitat (also a good sign that any surviving birds won't end up in an exhibit like the Florida birds).

Under-Appreciated Birds

Folks often mix these two guys up. Either way, they are often unwanted guests at the bird feeder. They can consume much seed and often show up in large numbers.

Both birds will keep your yard grub free if you let them. Grubs, beetle larvae that have hatched and feed on the roots of grass and plants, can be found close to the surface in late summer and early fall. Crows and grackles will nab them for you, eliminating the need for harmful pesticides.

The Common Grackle is much smaller than a crow, about robin size. At first glance, it appears to be black. In bright light, however, its beautiful purplish-green iridescence can be seen. It has a slim, pointy beak and bright yellow eyes. It may show up in large flocks numbering in the hundreds.

The American Crow is four times larger than a grackle. It is solid black. The beak of a crow is large and chunky compared to the slim, pointy beak of the grackle. Crows generally stay together in family groups and don't show up in large flocks like grackles.

Crows often get a bad rap, perhaps from years of landing the lead roles in every horror movie requiring a bird. A bunch of chickadees lined up on a fence post would not have looked nearly as initimidating in Alfred Hitchcock's "The Birds," as a bunch of crows. Even as cartoon characters crows are not portrayed correctly. They are often shown with yellow bills, yellow eyes, and yellow feet.

The American Crow is intelligent and has a highly developed communication system. It has adapted well to changes by humans to habitat and its numbers continue to do well in spite of attempts to hunt, poison and kill them to extinction.

Eastern Meadowlark

....and a Few More Back Yard Birds

The next few pages will show you even more birds you may see around your backyard, in a park, near a pond, in the woods, or near farmland. Again, the point being, that birds are everywhere for us to enjoy.

Put down the cell phone, grab a sketchbook, field guide or a camera or binoculars .... and take a look around. Document what you see. Enjoy what you see.

I've been told that my drawings are cute and endearing. One person told me that they possess a sweetness not found much any more. I admit, I do tend to give my birds, and all wildlife I draw, a personality. I can't seem to help it. My hope is that, if a person finds my illustration of a bird endearing, the feeling will transfer to the actual bird, starting a big chain reaction leading to a desire to protect birds, their habitat, and their environment.

The next bunch of illustrations were done to go with articles about each particular bird. For these, I tried to keep it real. I love the following drawings and am rather proud of them.

I'm not going to do alot of talking by each one, I'm simply going to let you enjoy them (at least I hope you will enjoy them). If you want to read about that bird, simply go to vvww.AskTheBirdFolks.com

Barn Swallows

Gray Catbird

Brown Creeper

Robin—baby

37

Tree Swallow

Wild Turkey

38

Cedar Waxwing

Yellow Warbler

Whip-poor-will

39

Bobolink

Eastern Phoebe

Fox Sparrow

40

Cliff Swallows

Ring-necked Pheasant

The odd egg in this nest belongs to a cowbird. The cowbird lets another bird hatch and raise its offspring by replacing one of the original eggs with one of its own.

Wood Pee-Wee

Budgies. Okay, you probably won't see these guys in your backyard, unless they escaped from a cage.

Hermit Thrush

Gray Jay

I love this drawing. It's another example of another bird shirking its parenting responsibilities, similar to what a Cowbird does.

The Yellow-billed and Black-billed Cuckoos occasionally lay an egg in another bird's nest. They are not as well known for this behavior as the Cowbird is, but it does happen.

The baby cuckoo grows rapidly and becomes active very early, usually resulting in the demise of the host bird's natural offspring.

The baby cuckoo is often much larger than its foster parent who works tirelessly to keep up with the feeding demands of its strange young.

Indigo Bunting

Common Redpolls

Winter Wren

Carolina Wren

47

Ovenbird

Yellow-headed Blackbird

48

Northern Bobwhite

BIRDS OF THE WATER

Green Heron

Everyone has access to body of water whether it be a pond, river, inland waterway, salt marsh, lake, or fresh water marsh. No matter which, there is bound to be a bird on it or along the edges of it. There is nothing more serene or calming than to watch a duck gliding quietly along a lake or a Great Blue Heron stalking fish at water's edge. Birds that make their living off the water are a diverse group, depending on us to keep their water clean and toxic chemicals out of their food.

GREAT BLUE HERON

The Great Blue Heron is the largest of the North American herons. It is abundant and common throughout North American and can be found along the edges all of bodies of water, both fresh and saltwater.

Its diet is also greatly varied, pretty much taking a stab at anything it comes across including insects, fish, turtles, frogs, rodents, snakes, and small birds. It mostly uses its sharp bill like scissors to grab prey, but is known too spear fish straight through, occasionally choking on one that turned out to be a tad too big.

Black-crowned Night Heron

Beginning a sketch of the Great Blue Heron makes use of all the basic shapes.

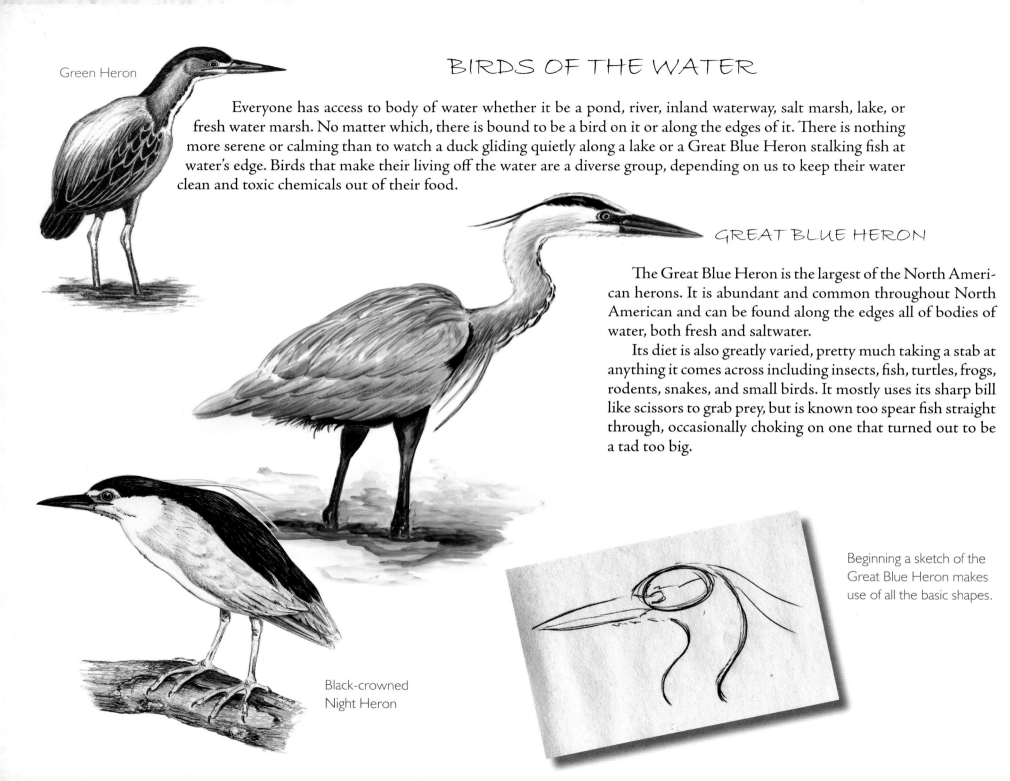

Standing at a height from 42 to 54 inches, the qreat Blue Heron is hard to miss. Even thought its numbers are abundant now, there was a time when populations quickly began to dwindle when folks with guns—not hunters mind you, just people with guns—could not resist using the Great Blue Heron for target practice.

Thanks to enforcement of bird protection laws, this practice was finally brought to a halt.

To observe herons and other water birds up close, I have found the best vantage point is from a kayak. I get to a certain point and stop paddinig and just let the kayak float. I have been surprised at how unperplexed they seem to be in the presence of a kayak. I never attempt to paddle right up to a heron or any bird for fear of startling it from its feeding or resting behavior.

Acrylic on slate.

Ducks & Geese

Waterfowl (this term usually refers to ducks, geese, and swans) probably has more history with people than any other group of birds and was the first group to be domesticated by humans. These birds are an ancient group with the oldest fossil remains dating back 80 million years. They live on every continent except Antarctica and every major island of the world.

These Red-breasted Mergansers are perfect examples of fish-eating ducks. They are slender and streamlined with powerful feet set way back on the body for speedy pursuit of underwater prey. The long, narrow bill is slightly serrated to grasp and hold onto a slippery fish. The wacky hairdo of both the male and female is hard to miss.

Observing and sketching ducks can be very rewarding. Start with the basic shapes than look for and add any dramatic markings often present, especially in the males.

The Common Eider is a great study with its dramatic black and white coloring. It is a robust sea duck which can be seen in waters off shore. It is a diving duck with a powerful bill that can crush the toughest mussels and crabs.

Talk about dramatic plumage. The drake (male) Wood Duck has few rivals. In fact, its Latin name translates to "betrothed" or "promised one" referring to the Wood Duck looking dressed and ready for a wedding ceremony.

The Wood Duck is a true perching duck, favoring secluded ponds and thick woods. It nests in tree cavities and will use a nest box.

Observing behavior can help to make an identification. The Common Goldeneye's bizarre courtship display of throwing its head back in a spray of water could help to ID this bird. This drawing was for an article about its crazy courting behavior.

The Harlequin probably rivals the Wood Duck for the title of "Most Dramatic Plumage." However, the Harlequin's Latin name translates to "clown." Not so lucky there. They seem to love rough water. Its population range is very limited. Lucky for me, we seem to get a few off Cape Cod in the winter.

The Mallard may very well be the most common, most recognized duck in the world. It is found throughout the Northern Hemisphere. Unfortunately for the Mallard, it is loved by hunters as a fast-flying target and for eating.

Mallards are dabbling ducks, often seen with their butts stuck up in the air and their heads underwater in a behavior called "tipping" while they feed on plants and seeds on the bottom of a body of shallow water.

There are many domesticated Mallards around that can be confused with wild Mallards. If a Mallard approaches you eyeing your Twinkie, chances are it is a domesticated duck. Wild Mallards are not as trusting

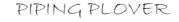

PIPING PLOVER

The Piping Plover is a great example of how even the smallest bird can make a difference. This little bird closes down prime beach areas to SUV's every peak tourist season. The beach is not closed to people, just to big SUV and truck tires which have a tendency to squash the small baby birds.

Thanks to conservation efforts and the kind understanding of beachgoing enthusiasts, the Piping Plover is finally making a comeback.

The illustration, left, not only appeared with an article in the newspaper; but was also used for plover conservation signs on Prince Edward Island.

The illustration, right, was done in watercolor the painting, left, was acrylic on roofing slate.

56

This painting was done with acrylic on slate. Definitely falls into the "cute" category. This was one of a series of paintings for my recently published children's book "Chickadee & The Whale. "

BLACK-BELLIED PLOVER

For an article about Black-bellied Plovers. Also not weird or whacky, but I left it out by mistake back in the "water" section. A striking bird when seen in breeding plumage. Article Date: 07/13/07

ATLANTIC PUFFIN

A popular sight on wildlife and whale watching trips off Maine, the Atlantic Puffin nests in burrows in the ground or crevices in the rocks. This protects them from their chief predator, the Black-backed Gull. However, in places where rats or cats (remember this for later) have been introduced, their populations can be adversely affected.

Some birds, like these Wilson's Storm-Petrels, can only be seen by going on a whale watch.

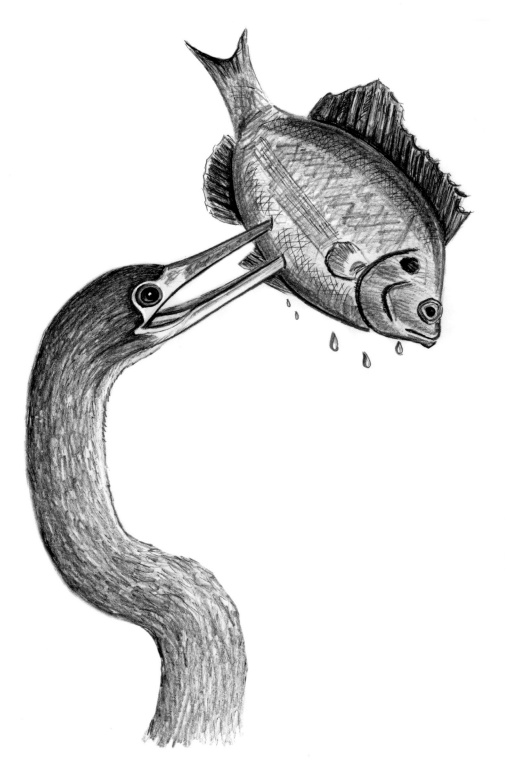

One way to help you identify a bird is by looking at its beak. The long pointy beaks of the Anhinga, left, and the Great Egret, right, provide a good clue that these guys are capable of spearing fish for dinner.

62

GREAT BLACK-BILLED GULL

The Great Black-backed Gull is an impressive sight. Reaching a length of up to 31 inches, it is the largest of our gull species. It will eat anythIng and everything, including the eggs and chicks of other sea birds. In areas with access to dumps, landfills and the occasional French fry, its numbers can become quite large, as can Herring Gull populations.

When I worked as naturalist on a whale watch boat, we would pile supplies on the dock for loading. I had the opportunity to see a Black-backed Gull about to take of with an entire sealed metal rack of twenty-four muffins. Not a light load. I was tempted to let him have it, but felt that all of the hydrogenated vegetable oil and sugar in that many muffns would not do him any good, not to mention the plastic wrapping.

GREATER FLAMINGO

The Greater Flamingo uses its large, whacky-looking beak for straining tiny plants, animals and fish from the water, not unlike the way baleen whales strain zoo-plankton and small fish from the water.

OSPREY

The Osprey is the symbol of conservation success. It rang the alarm on the effect that the use of DDT was having on wildlife. Osprey eggs became so fragile, they would break before hatching. The bird almost became extinct.

Thanks to the banning of DDT and the introduction of manmade platforms where the birds could nest, they have made a thriving comeback, especially on Cape Cod where I live.

Osprey will return to the same nest year after year, adding sticks and whatever else it fancies. Nests can become quite large.

Their fishing skills are supreme, sighting and soaring down on a fish from as high as 100 feet with it talons outstretched.

OWLS

EASTERN SCREECH OWL

The Eastern Screech Owl will move into your backyard if you have the right habitat and put up a wooden nest box designed for screech owls.

The screech owl takes advantage of a variety of food including mice, other small mammals, insects, snakes and even other birds. It is even capable of catching fish and frogs.

SNOWY OWL

This illustration was for an article about a sighting of a Snowy on Cape Cod. Unlike most owls that hunt at night, the Snowy Owl hunts by day.

Seeing one is certainly a striking sight. It is not unusual, but not common either (figure that one out) to see a Snowy Owl where I live.

Recently, someone reported coming home to find a Snowy Owl on his roof, a favorite vantage point of this owl.

This Snowy was painted on a canoe paddle, of all things, which I then scanned into the computer for use as a print.

GREAT HORNED OWL

The Great Horned Owl hunts at night. It flies without a sound and sees and hears with unmatched ability. This owl will take down the usual squirrel and rabbit. But it will also hunt other birds: geese, songbirds, ducks, and hawks. It is one of the few predators that will hunt skunks and porcupines. Basically, short of a 747, anything is fair game to the Great Horned, including loose house cats allowed to roam about at night. Because of the wide variety of prey this owl will choose from, it has the nickname of the "Flying Tiger."

The drawing below was done for an article about "mobbing" behavior. These crows are attempting to drive the owl away before it gets any idea of making a meal of them. If you hear a loud ruckus of birds, take a closer look. They may be targeting a Great Horned Owl.

The drawing was put together using the owl left, the crow earlier in this book, one tree, and one branch then assembled on the computer.

This painting was done with acrylic
on a piece of roofing slate.

BARRED OWL

Most articles about owls are written in an attempt to identify a call someone heard at night. The Barred Owl's signature call, "Who-cooks-for-you, who-cooks-for-you-all," is easy to recognize.

This owl is capable of a bizarre variety of sounds, however, worthy of any horror film, especially when heard in the deep, swampy habitats where it likes to hang out.

Time was short and I only had time for these quick sketches. Every article illustration is done the morning it is due (talk about pressure). Sometimes stuff happens and you just have to go with it.

BARN OWL

The Barn Owl lives among people in barns and buildings and is probably most responsible for scarry ghost stories. With its ghostly white face and white outspread wings, it can be a creepy sight in the dark. It has its own screeching call to make one shiver.

BURROWING OWL

The yearly April Fool's article is my favorite one to illustrate. Some-body always falls for it. The Burrowing Owl lives in burrows in the ground in the western plains and southern Florida. This article stated that Burrowing Owls had moved into the dunes of Provincetown, Massachu-setts, at the base of wind turbines being erected out there, and only time would tell if the birds stayed when construction resumed on April 1.

To read this entire article, go to www.AskTheBirdFolks.com, which is dated 03/31/06.

A Few Other Birds Of Prey

NORTHERN HARRIER

AMERICAN KESTREL

COOPER'S HAWK

Bald Eagle after a Red-breasted Merganser, painted for an article about the speed of birds.

Predators of the Back Yard...Real & Imagined

Enjoy all the wildlife that comes to your yard. Squirrels, chipmunks, and other wildlife don't know that the seed you put out is only for the birds.

There are plently of ways to keep these guys off your bird feeder. Staff at a real birding shop can help you pick out what will work for your yard. Other visitors will still be attracted to your yard, however.

If you're going to lose sleep over this or reach for a shotgun, don't put a feeder out at all.

Look at these faces. Cute enough to make you want to feed them too? There are many squirrel-proof feeders on the market now that do work and baffles that will keep chipmunks off.

The Red Fox eats quite a varied fare including the usual assortment of small mammals, such as mice, voles, rabbits and even the occasional, dreaded bird-seed-eating squirrel. But it also eats nuts, berries, and bird eggs.

This illustration was done for a question about foxes stealing and hiding eggs. Yes they do. Foxes are known to hide any of their food items to save for "a rainy day." They are even known to go back and dig up an item, as if checking to make sure it is still there, and then hide it again.

If you put out suet in a suet cage and the whole thing mysteriously keeps disappearing, you can be sure there is a raccoon behind the theft. They're known for this behavior. It's what they do.

The suet cage must be fastened to a tree with a chain, brought in at night, or hung on a branch that will not support the raccoon's weight.

Raccoons will also raid bird feeders and birdhouses. Keeping these guys out is a bit trickier than keeping out squirrels, but it can be done. There is such a thing as a raccoon baffle that can be placed on a pole under a feeder or birdhouse to keep the raccoon from climbing up.

CLARK

The White-Footed Mouse will use an empty birdhouse during the winter to make a nest and to keep warm. It will also help itself to bird seed.

This is the real predator of the backyard.

Loose house cats and feral cats kill an estimated five million (5,000,000!) native songbirds every day. Every day! That's five million cardinals, chickadees, quail, bluebirds, to name a few. Many folks will say, "Not my Fluffy!" Statistics show otherwise.

Cats allowed to roam are being exposed to feline leukemia, ticks carrying lyme disease, and the ever-present automobile. And remember the "Flying Tiger" mentioned earlier? The domestic cat is no match for a Great Horned Owl. A loose cat stalking about at night will make for a quick snack to a Great Horned.

A bell on the collar doesn't work. A cat learns very quickly to move without jingling it.

In some areas, like here on Cape Cod, songbirds have a new hero in town. A predator whose cunning surpasses that of the domestic house cat and whose dens are decorated with cat collars ... the Eastern Coyote. To learn about the importance of coyotes to the balance of the ecosystem, visit: www.easterncoyoteresearch.com.

Many cities and towns are beginning to adopt leash laws for cats. Would you let your horse, goat, or guinea pig wander over to your neighbor's yard and kill things? Then why should a cat be allowed to?

THE WACKY, WEIRD, & EXOTIC BIRDS

The next bunch of pages are illustrations done of unusual birds for unusual questions. To read more of the corresponding article, go to: www/AskTheBirdFolks.com.

This illustration was for a question about how many bird species there are.
Article date: 04/06/07

This is a Red-crested Cardinal. A person on a trip to Hawaii saw one there. It was introduced to Hawaii, but native to South America. About ten years ago, one was photographed on a feeder in Massachusetts. It was probably a bird that escaped from a cage.
Article date: 04/13/07

The question for this article began with a story about a Sandhill Crane that imprinted on a horse. I was very excited about drawing a horse. When baby birds hatch, they are wired to follow the first moving creature they see.
Article date: 06/01/07

83

South America

This was about about the rising cost of bird seed, due to several reasons...the demand for sunflower oil for healthier snacks, the demand for growing corn for ethanol, and the high cost of gas to transport the seed.
Article date: 04/19/07

Someone wondered about birds migrating from South America. They don't. Not really. Native South American birds pretty much stay put.
Article date: 07/20/07

This drawing went with an article about where the birding was better, Australia or New Zealand. The picture pretty much says it all. Just in case, the answer was not New Zealand.
Article date: 10/13/06

The Fulmar is an example of a sea bird with
a tube-like structure on the beak to expel salt
from its system quickly and efficiently.
Article date: 10/27/06

This was a very special illustration. It went with a question from a serviceman on a tour of duty in Kabul, Afghanistan, about the introduction of mayna birds to various countries for pest control. His family regularly sent him the "Ask the Bird Folks" articles clipped from the paper.
Article date: 07/15/05

A question came from the island of Guam asking why there were so few bird species there. The drawing, right, shows the reason, the Brown Tree Snake. No one knows how it was introduced, but it made quick work of the native bird population. A tourist destination for snake-lovers, Guam has an estimated 14,000 snakes per square mile.
Article date: 10/07/05

A European Goldfinch was sighted in a yard upstate. Most definitely it was a lucky escapee from a birdcage.
Article date: 12/09/05

"She Wore a Dead Bird on Her Head"

I was just looking through my pile of calendars from a host of different conservation groups with pictures of polar bears, whales, dolphins, wolves, sea turtles, sharks, otters, tigers, elephants, the planet ... all needing to be saved. It felt overwhelming and it made me feel like crying. Then I got to this drawing and it reminded me of the story behind it. I felt better. "She Wore a Dead Bird on Her Head" was a book written by Kathryn Lasky about the start of the Massachusetts Audubon Society. This drawing was for an article about that story.

In 1886 a New York ornithologist stood on a New York City street and counted 170 dead birds adorning the hats of the ladies walking by.

In 1896 two women, Harriet Hemenway and her cousin, Minnie Hall, decided to do something about it. This was a time when women did not have much power. They could not even vote yet. These women of Boston influenced their powerful husbands that watching birds alive in trees was better than watching them dead on hats. Thus started the first group to promote watching and protecting native birds, the Massachusetts Audubon Society.

These women went on to spread the word that it was no longer fashionable to kill birds for hats and rang the alarm on mass killing of native birds. Other Audubon Societies began springing up everywhere. The first act to protect birds came in 1900, followed by the most important, The Migratory Bird Act, in 1913.

Many native bird species were headed for extinction. Two women in 1896 were able to put a stop to it.

If you have a pile of calendars like I do, pick one. Pick a cause, any cause. Write a letter, take some action, get involved, donate. You never know what might happen.

Article date: 03/11/05.

This drawing was done for an article about choosing a field guide. There are plenty of good ones on the market. If getting one for all of North America seems a bit intimidating, choose one for Eastern North America. But get one. Folks try to get by with a field guide for "beginners" or a limited fold-out poster type. These usually prove to be too limiting pretty quickly.
Article date: 06/10/05

This drawing was a total joke about bird watching attire. Basically, it's a no brainer, plain and neutral is the way to go.
Article date: 7/29/05

Who eats fiddler crabs? Whimbrels for one. Glossy Ibises for another, and crows and gulls if they can catch them.
Article date: 11/04/05

Following the movie, "March of the Penguins,"
questions about Emperor Penguins and penguins
in general were all the rage.
Article date: 08/05/05

I picked Gintoo Penguins, below, for a question about
whether or not penguins have knees. They do.
Article Date: 09/26/05

92

Canada Geese in large numbers can cause problems in
some areas. An enterprising local woman built a business
around this problem ... using trained Border Collies to
drive them away.
Article Date: 02/09/0l

The Great Auk, once abundant, was hunted to extinction by early Europeans. When the last pair of Auks were discovered in 1844, they were killed and the last egg destroyed. Nice. (Time to go back and read the Audubon story again.)

Passenger Pigeons once numbered in the billions. It was killed by the flockloads to extinction. It only took 22 years for billions to turn into 0.
Article Date: 11/02/07

Okay, time to get funny again. A person put mothballs in a garden to keep pests out. Grackles were observed rubbing the mothballs on their feathers. Many bird species rub ants along their feathers,. It's thought that the formic acid from the ants helps to rid and repel parasites. This behavior is called "anting." It's amazing that the birds figured out that an ant or a mothball would be useful for anything..
Article Date: 08/11/06

This drawing went with an article about bird phobias. Who could possibly be afraid of these sweet faces?
Article Date: 10/26/07

A question about bird migration prompted me to piece together lots of previously completed illustrations. I like the colorized herons here, in the newspaper they appeared black and white.
Article Date: 10/06/06

96

Neither weird nor whacky, however, the American Avocet is not a common sight where I live.
Article Date: 12/28/07

97

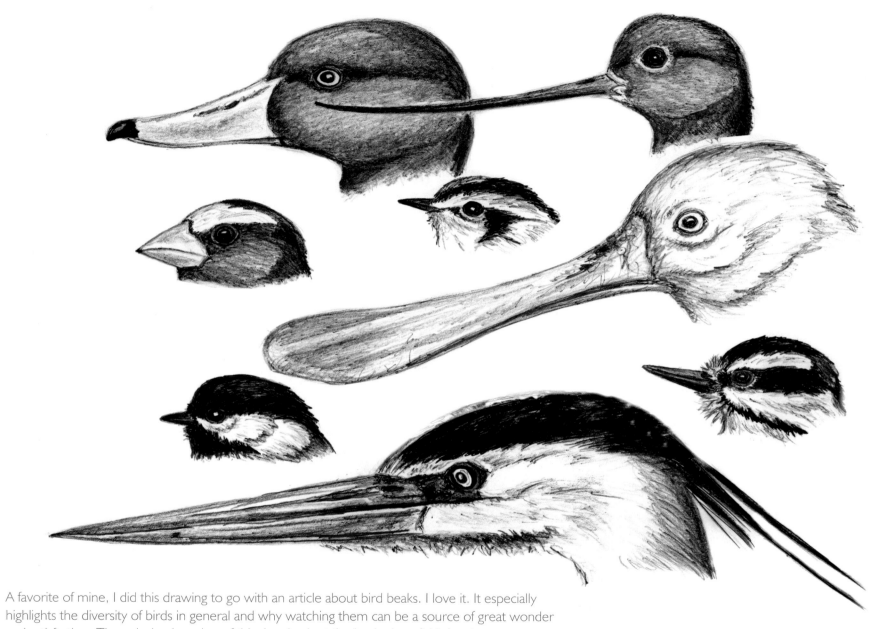

A favorite of mine, I did this drawing to go with an article about bird beaks. I love it. It especially highlights the diversity of birds in general and why watching them can be a source of great wonder and satisfaction. The colorized version of this drawing is at the beginning of this book.
Article Date: 11/05/04

Chickadee with Daisies. Painted with acrylic on roofing slate.

MORE PAINTINGS

Canada Goose. A commissioned work painted on a wooden canoe paddle. I placed the painted paddle right on the scanner and scanned it into the computer. I was then able to make prints and note cards from the same image. The client wanted to use this image for his Christmas cards.

A miniature beaver painting done in watercolor and pencil. The chickadees are from the chickadees and willow painting earlier in this book. The cardinal is from the mill scene right.

White-breasted Nuthatch, Northern Cardinal. and Downy Woodpecker. Acrylic on canvas paper.

White-breasted Nuthatch.
Acrylic on slate.

Loon with baby, acrylic on canvas paper.

Black-capped Chickadee.
Acrylic on slate

Great Blue Heron, Snowy Egret,
and Black-crowned Night Heron.
Acrylic on canvas paper.

Wood Duck, acrylic on slate.

Northern Cardinal and Ruby-throated Hummingbird.
Both done in acrylic on slate.

Colored pencil and pen.

Acrylic on slate.

I love Great Blue Herons and I love this painting. Most of the time I paint to please myself, after discovering it's really the only way I can paint. I figure that if I like it, someone else in the world should like it too. I'm not trying to be the next Roger Tory Peterson and get every feather absolutely right on. Sometimes I want to, though, just to show myself that I can. I think I did hit it right on with this heron.

This was done acrylic on a gallery-wrapped canvas (which means you paint the edges and it does not need to be framed). I hate framing and I'll do anything to avoid it. For another, I like the feeling that the scene keeps going beyond the edges of the canvas.

Bald Eagle, acrylic on slate. Painting on slate is another way to get out of framing, plus I like the smooth surface.

Common Loon, also on slate.

Acrylic on canvas.

Snowman and birds in
acrylic on slate.

Thanks for taking a look at this book. I hope you learned something about birds. I hope you're inspired to grab some binoculars and go for a walk, go to a local bird club meeting, or go on a whale watch or even an adventure trip. Join your local Audubon Society. Put up a bird feeder. Take out a sketch pad.

Better yet, in your next batch of mail, pick out one wildlife or conservation group looking for help. You know there'll be one. Pick one, any one. They all need help and they're all doing good work. It just takes one person at a time to make a difference.

www.CatherineClarkStudio.com